MW00560289

JOURNAL

PETER PAUPER PRESS, INC.
WHITE PLAINS, NEW YORK

PETER PAUPER PRESS
Fine Books and Gifts Since 1928

OUR COMPANY

In 1928, at the age of twenty-two, Peter Beilenson began printing books on a small press in the basement of his parents' home in Larchmont, New York. Peter—and later, his wife, Edna—sought to create fine books that sold at "prices even a pauper could afford."

Today, still family owned and operated, Peter Pauper Press continues to honor our founders' legacy—and our customers' expectations—of beauty, quality, and value.

This journal's cover replicates a gilded lacquer 19th-century bookbinding for an illuminated Persian manuscript. An artist created the lacquerwork design with layered paint, shellac sanded to a shine, and gold leaf.

The original binding houses *Yusuf and Zulaykha*, a Persian-language illuminated manuscript in the collection of The Walters Art Museum, late 12th century AH/AD 18th century (Mughal), W.646.

Copyright © 2021
Peter Pauper Press, Inc.
202 Mamaroneck Avenue
White Plains, NY 10601 USA
All rights reserved
ISBN 978-1-4413-3599-9
Printed in China
7 6 5 4 3

Visit us at www.peterpauper.com

I have helped my family clean-up on christmas